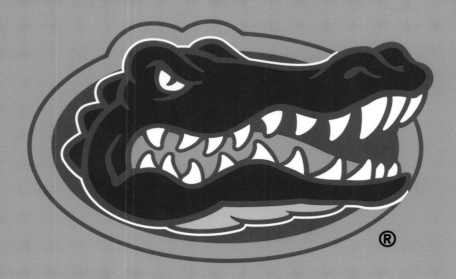

"To the children of the Gator Nation both young and old may your heart always beat Orange and Blue and always stay Gator true."

~Mark "Dr. D" Damohn

"To my wife Helene and our children Lauren, Thea, and Nathan whose unflagging patience, inspiration and support have made my creative career possible."

~Gene Hotaling

"To all children with whom our future rests, dream well and always do your best"

~Michele Leilani
www.michelesphotorestorations.com

UNIVERSITY OF FLORIDA, FLORIDA, GATORS, FLORIDA GATORS, U OF F, FIGHTING GATORS and THE SWAMP are trademarks of the University of Florida and are used under license.

ISBN: 978-1-936319-18-3

PRT1114B

Printed in the United States

THE GATOR ABC BOOK

GO GATORS!

NATIONAL CHAMPIONS
1996 2006 2008

BEN HILL GRIFFIN STADIUM

Written by
Mark "Dr. D" Damohn

Illustrated by
Gene Hotaling

is for Albert and Alberta

Who love to cheer

For Gator fans far

And Gator fans near.

They are the great Florida Mascots.

In The Swamp they will be here.

**B** is for Ben Hill Griffin Stadium

And the Pride of the Sunshine Band.

Whose great music

Is the pride of the Florida land.

 is for cheerleaders

Who cheer and make noise.

They help bring spirit

To our Orange and Blue Boys.

 is for defense

Who stand like a stonewall.

It makes the opponents

Turn over the ball.

 is for embrace.

For our defense will race

To put the opponents on the ground

And back in their place.

 is for Florida.

The home of the Gators.

There are none that are greater

Than these great Florida Gators.

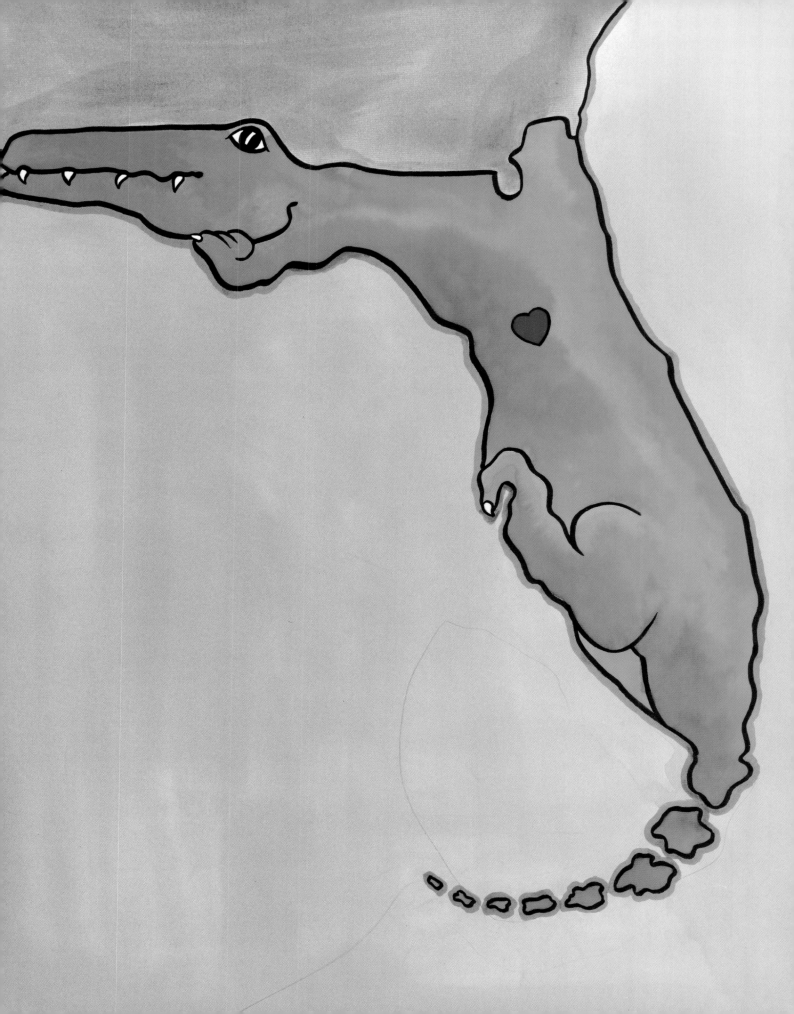

 **G** is for the Game Day Gators.

On Saturdays our troubles

We pack away

And head to The Swamp on the double.

 is for half time

It's time for a snack.

Time to get a hot dog and soft drink.

Knowing our boys will soon be back.

 is for Ice

These Gators are cool.

The opponents arrive

But they leave like fools.

 is for Jumbotron

The Gators score time-after-time

On the big-screen we see the score.

The Gators are in rhythm and rhyme.

 **K** is for kicking

Extra points and Field Goals.

With so many points

We are happy Gator souls.

We are rocking this joint!

is for lining up over the ball.

Which way will it go?

Gators are smart.

They already know.

M is for motor home
For going all the way to The Swamp
For making a great road trip.
The Gators put on such a romp.

is for being best in the nation
Championships have been won
But the Gators are still hungry.
The Gators are not done.

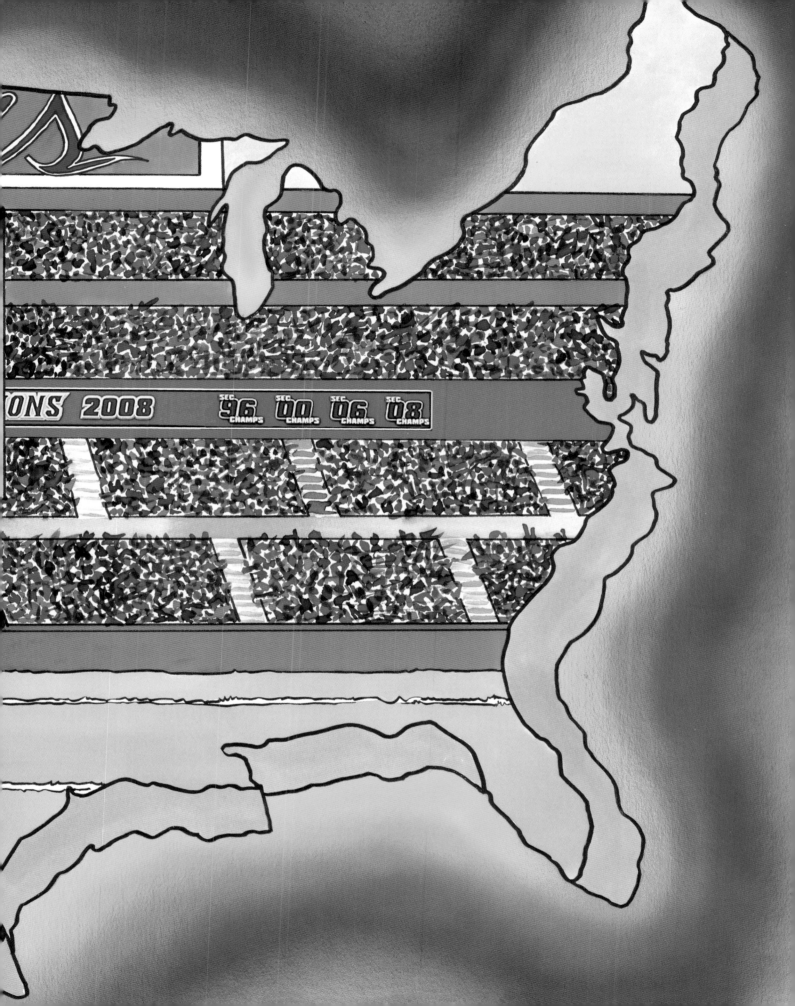

is for "Oh My !!!"

That is what the Gators like to say.

It's so amazing.

What another great play.

P is for plays of great passing

That will be talked about for many a day.

The players and fans have so much fun.

They would not have it any other way.

Q is for quarters, 15 minutes long.

The Gators love to play football

When the weather is cool

And the season is Fall.

R is for reptile.
The Gators are in style.
Guaranteed to place a smile
And make the fans go wild.

S is for Swamp Spirit
Albert, Alberta, and the fans
Make the crowds roar.
OH MY !!!
The Gators made another score.

 is for team

Of these Gators we are very fond.

The fans yell and scream.

 The Gators have such a strong bond.

 is for university

Players and fans

Being a Gator

Isn't it simply grand?

is for victory

That's what the Gators expect.

It's not surprising...

Since our opponents are decked.

is for winning

Game-after-game.

The opponents are all different,

But the results are still the same.

is for excitement.

That's what the fans want to see.

The Gators scoring lots of points.

Points are made for you and for me.

is for Yankee Doodle

And uncle Sam

You are his niece or nephew

And you live in this American land.

 is for zebra

Nickname of the officials.

They keep the game honest

By blowing their whistles.

You have finished reading the book.

You have reached the end.

Albert and Alberta say thanks for the look.

They say make sure you share it with a friend.